THE
"NO HYPE"
GUIDE
TO GETTING STARTED
WORKING
FROM HOME

Put These Proven Secrets To Work
& <u>You</u> Can Escape The Rat Race Too...

DAN WIGGS

ISBN-13: 978-1516983223

ISBN-10: 151698322X

earndifferent.com

TIP: All the URLs referenced in this book can be found at earndifferent.com/links

Contents

About The Author 1

Part 1: 7
Getting Started 7
Pros and Cons 9
Your Office Setup 15
Helpful Software 21
Pro Tips..27

Part 2: Your 10 Step Plan 37
Step 1: Plan Your Knowledge 39
Step 2: Plan Your Mindset...49
Step 3: Prepare Your Family..53
Step 4: Plan Your Branding 61
Step 5: Plan Your List Building 69
Step 6: Plan to Be of Service First...............................77
Step 8: Plan to Tap Into Affiliate Marketing Earnings..........95
Step 9: Plan to Include Ad Revenue in Your Business 103
Step 10: Plan Your Traffic 109

Conclusion 121

BONUS: The "High Commission" Secrets Of A Work From Home Millionaire MP3 123

Resources 127

About The Author

My name's Dan Wiggs and I've probably been in your shoes (that is, if you have struggled to find a way to succeed online!)

I setup **earndifferent.com** to carve a path through the hypey get rich quick crap that floods our inboxes every day.

It's my mission to find, rate and share the proven training and online business opportunities that actually will help give you the luxury of working from home - and not just waste your precious time and hard earned money.

I really do want to help.

So that's why I'm sharing my experience and knowledge with you in three ways…

The first one you know about – it's this book!

Secondly, you've got The Earn Different Top 10 Sources Of Online Income (earndifferent.com/top10) – this is 100% free to readers of this book.

And lastly, my free email newsletter – regular tips and training and freebies (earndifferent.com)

But first a little more about me…

Turning back the clock to 2012 - I was desperate to escape my tedious job in property maintenance.

I really wanted to make money on the internet from my own home, rather than unblocking toilets in stranger's apartment blocks.

I had tried countless online systems.

Some of them worked ok, but the majority didn't make me a bean.

In 2011 I dabbled in publishing on Amazon's Kindle, and soon had a string of number 1 non-fiction best sellers (many of which still make sales on a daily basis even now).

But it was only at the start of 2013, that it finally dawned on me - I needed to find a mentor - and to stop chasing after every shiny object and every IM fad.

I have learned one hell of a lot since then – entered the crazy world of copywriting, created information products, built a faithful list of subscribers that grows daily, forged solid business relationships - and have made some excellent friends too.

Now I spend a couple of hours a day writing emails, researching new work from home products, checking out Facebook, and making a full-time, monthly recurring income.

And you know what is even better?

I don't have to commute.

I don't have to miss a moment of my kids growing up.

And I get to see them every day before they go to school and am there to greet them on their return.

I don't have to work a crappy job just to pay for childcare.

I can take the dogs for a walk when I want to, go to the gym when it suits me, work the hours I choose.

It's bloody marvellous!

So if you want to discover steady sources of online income, and to do it right the first time - check out my Top 10 at earndifferent.com/top10, and keep an eye out for my emails.

To your success!

Dan Wiggs

London, England

Introduction

Have you ever dreamed about working from home?

More and more people make the switch every year, and this trend is not likely to stop anytime soon.

If your job mostly involves working on a computer there is really no need to drive into an actual office every day, since you can do the same thing just as well from your own house.

Whether you're still only dreaming about it, or you've already made the transition, working from home brings a few questions and challenges that must be overcome in order to stay productive and make the most out of it.

From the way your home office is setup to the software you use on your computer, there are many things to consider. Here are some of the things you'll learn in this book:

- *The pros and cons of working from home (believe it or not, there are not only advantages to it)*
- *What kind of equipment you need in your office, and what you need to think about when it comes to your office environment and atmosphere*
- *How the right software can make you more productive and solve many of the little problems that can pop up when you're working from home*
- *Why keeping a routine and a set schedule makes sense for many home workers (even if it's not exactly what they dreamed about...)*

- *How to combat the potential loneliness and isolation that working from home can bring*
- *Why it's important to not let work spill over into your free time, and how you can ensure you keep your work and private lives separate even if they take place in the same location*
- *How to keep your mind and body healthy and productive*
- *How to avoid distractions and allow for focused, productive work in your home office*

...and much more!

Part 1:

Getting Started

Pros and Cons

Few things are completely black and white in life, and working from home is no different. While there are certainly many advantages to it, there are also quite a few potential pitfalls that you need to be aware of before making the transition. In this chapter we'll go over some of them. Note that the impact of some of the cons can be significantly reduced with the right methods - more about that in the "Pro Tips" chapter later on.

Pros

Set your own hours

Unless you have clients requiring you to be reachable between certain hours, you're free to set your own hours. If you want to start working at 6 PM and work all through the night, no one will object. If you have errands to run, you can do it in the middle of the week when everyone else is busy with work.

No commuting

Many people spend dozens of hours every week just traveling to/from work. Not only is it frustrating to be forced to spend that much time in a car or on a train, but it's also expensive. Working from home does away with commuting completely, giving you more free time to spend as you choose.

Fewer interruptions

It's generally easier to get into "the zone" and work completely interrupted when you're working from home than in a busy office environment where everyone seems to want to interact with you. This is at least true if you're alone while working; if you have a spouse, children or even pets around you may experience the complete opposite!

Less stressful

If you're good at noticing the signs when you're becoming stressed out, it's generally easier to curb these feelings when you're working from home. You can take a step back at any time and do something relaxing to lower your stress levels.

Location independent

While it's called working from *home*, usually you're free to do your work from anywhere you please. If you want to work from your favorite café, or even from a luxury resort in Thailand, go ahead and do it! Most people, however, find that they work best from their own home in something resembling an actual office.

Saves money

Just by removing the need for commuting you'll save tons of money every month. No need for expensive work-appropriate clothes. Add to that less money spent on eating out and working from home may be the best thing that's happened to your wallet in quite a while.

Easier to stay healthy (but discipline is required)

As you set your own hours you're free to hit up the gym every day, or make it a habit to go for a long walk at lunchtime. You'll generally be free to cook your own meals, meaning you could go for something healthy. However, no one will be there to push you so you need to stay disciplined if you want your healthy habits to become permanent.

Cons

More distractions

At home you'll probably find enough distractions around you to easily keep yourself occupied every single hour of the day, should you want to. From video games and watching TV to simply napping the day away, the temptations are many and you must stay disciplined if you want to keep working from home.

Can feel isolated

When you work in an office some social interaction is part of the job. When you get home after a long day it can feel real good to shut the door and enjoy the silence. When you're working from home the opposite is often true. You'll get limited (or no) social interaction during your work hours, so at the end of the day you may want to stay socially active to stave off the feelings of loneliness.

Harder to keep your business and private life separate

Another advantage of office life is that once you go home at the end of the day, you can put your work out of your mind. That's not necessarily true when you're working from home, when your computer is *right there* and you can check your mail even if it's 11 PM and you should be in bed.

Takes up physical space

Most people who work from home find that they need a dedicated office to stay focused, meaning you may need to sacrifice some living space (or get a larger home with a spare room to use as an office).

It's not all savings

To be productive at home you may find that you need to do some initial investing. At the very least you'll need a good computer, a printer and a fast Internet connection. Some of these you may be able to write off as business expenses, but probably not all. Of course, if you already have these things in place before starting this is not an issue.

Less competitive environment = less motivation?

Some people may find that they need a competitive environment to stay productive, while others do just fine motivating themselves. The latter category may find it a lot easier to work from home.

Technical issues

What happens when your Internet connection goes down? Most likely you'll be left rolling your thumbs waiting for it to come back online. In an office environment this is less likely to happen as there are often tech support people handling these issues quickly, whereas at home you may be stuck for days waiting for your Internet provider to send out a technician.

Chores increasing stress levels

When you're working from home you just can't help but notice when the house needs vacuuming, or the dishes are piling up in the sink. This can actually be very stressful, dragging you down mentally. However, doing chores when you really should be working is not a great idea either. It can be hard to find a good balance in this area, even after years of working from home.

Easier to stagnate professionally

Working in an office you can't help but get at least some industry news and pick up some new skills through co-workers. You may even be sent off on courses to learn new skills. When you work from home, however, you'll have to continually develop your skills yourself, and strive to stay up-to-date on the latest developments so you're not stagnating.

Takeaways

- *One of the main benefits of working from home is the flexibility and ability to choose yourself when, where and how you work*
- *You need to be a self-starter with the ability to stay disciplined and focused on your own to get the best results*
- *Working from home can allow you to both save money and live a healthy lifestyle, but if you aren't careful it can also lead to the complete opposite*
- *Separating your working life from your private life is one of the main challenges when you're working from home, and something you need to actively strive to prevent*

Your Office Setup

It should go without saying that you need a good home office if you're going to work from home. Not only do you need it to have the right size and properties, you also need to outfit it with the proper equipment. Let's go over what you need:

Equipment

Computer (and software)

Regardless of what kind of work you do, you're going to need a reasonably modern computer. It doesn't have to be a state-of-the-art gaming PC though, and in most cases $500 will be plenty to buy one that will last at least a couple of years. Of course if you work with graphics or other resource intensive tasks you may have to spend a bit more.

Also, don't forget to budget for the software you need. Again this is highly dependent on what you do, but most people working from home will need at least a working office suite. There are free alternatives available, such as Open Office (installs on your computer) and Google Docs (cloud-based), which may or may not work depending on your needs.

Scanner and printer

While we're moving more and more towards the "paperless society", the truth is you still need a printer to have a fully functioning home office. It doesn't have to be anything fancy, a cheaper black & white laser printer will do just fine for office use (unless you think you'll need to print color documents). You can get by without a scanner, but it can be real handy if you need to, for example, sign and e-mail a contract. You may be able to take a photo of it with your phone instead, but keep in mind that the quality will be much worse and the other party may not accept it.

Internet connection

No doubt you're going to need a reasonably fast Internet connection, but it's even more important that it's reliable. The last thing you want is an Internet connection that comes and goes, leaving you cut off from the world and completely unproductive while waiting for it to come back. The fact is you may not even be able to live in some places where Internet connectivity is poor, unless you're prepared to put up with the annoyance a flakey connection will bring.

Most work related tasks do not *require* a fast connection, but if you know you're often downloading large documents or working with streaming video, it will be worth spending a few extra bucks for top-tier speeds.

Desk and chair

This is one area where many people go the cheapest possible route and end up regretting it later on. Assuming you spend around 8 hours in front of your computer every day, it really pays off to invest in an ergonomic work space. Cheap desk chairs may actually end up hurting you in the long run, and you have to ask yourself if the money you save is actually worth the toll it takes on your health. A good chair may cost around $400 and up, but where a cheap chair may break after just a year or two, a good chair will often last for at least 5 years and sometimes more.

Aside from a good chair you may also want to invest in a desk you can raise to standing height. Many health problems are caused by being locked in a single position all day long, and switching between sitting and standing can be very helpful to combat that. It is not recommended for most people to stick to *only* standing, as it may just shift the problems from the back/shoulders to the hips/knees/feet.

The ideal environment

Quiet

While some people have no trouble working in a noisy environment, most find it very distracting when they're trying to be productive. If you're one of them, make sure your home office can provide you with the peace and quiet you need, or you may find it difficult to get anything done. If there are other people in the house, make sure they understand and respect your needs. At the very least you'll need a door you can shut when you find yourself too distracted by the outside world.

Free from distractions

If you know you have difficulties staying disciplined, it may not be the best idea to have a TV or video game in your office. The temptation may be great to "just take a quick break" and before you know it several hours have passed. Ideally you'll want to keep your home office outfitted strictly for work and nothing else.

Good lighting

It is not to be underestimated how important good lighting is for your work environment, especially in the winter months when natural lighting doesn't amount to much. Everyone has their own preferences when it comes to lighting, and you may have to experiment a bit to find the best setup for your needs. If you're a person that tends to have low energy in the winter months, consider adding an SAD lamp to your arsenal and keep it on in the mornings.

Comfortable climate

It may go without saying that keeping a comfortable indoor climate is important in your home office. Regardless of where you live, you may find that your office gets too hot in the summers, in which case it may be worth spending some cash on an air conditioner. In the winter you may find the indoor climate too dry, which is easily fixed by a good-quality air humidifier.

Takeaways

- *You don't need a super expensive computer to work from home, and much of the software you can use is available for free*
- *A reliable Internet connection is an absolute must*
- *Spending some money on a good chair and desk is a wise investment, because it allows you to comfortably work all day without pain*
- *Make sure your home office has good atmosphere and, if possible, located in a quiet area that's free from distractions*

Helpful Software

There is a multitude of software out there designed to make working easier and more efficient. In this chapter we'll go over some of the most widely praised programs, some free and some paid, that can help you boost your productivity and make working from home a breeze.

Instant Communication: Skype
(earndifferent.com/skype)

In the last few years, Skype has become the #1 instant communication tool for online workers. Whether you prefer instant messaging, phone calls or video chat, Skype offers it all for free (or, in some situations, for a low fee). It's available for most platforms, and you can even take it with you in your phone or tablet.

Office Suite: Microsoft Office (or similar)

(earndifferent.com/office)

There's no way around it: if you're going to work from home you need an office suite. Microsoft Office remains industry standard, but there are lots of alternatives available if you're feeling experimental. There are cloud-based solutions like Google Docs (free) as well as locally installed software such as Open Office (free) and Apple Productivity Apps/iWork (commercial). All of the alternatives are file-format compatible with

Microsoft Office, but not all formatting features are supported by them.

Cloud Storage: Dropbox (earndifferent.com/dropbox)

Dropbox is cloud-based storage that lets you store your work files online and reach them wherever you are. You can install it on all your computers, phones and tablets, ensuring your important documents are always with you (assuming you have an Internet connection at least sporadically so it can sync). It's also great when you're collaborating with others, as you can share folders and files with them and see whenever a file is changed.

Project Management: Basecamp

(earndifferent.com/basecamp)

There's no shortage of great project management tools on the web, but Basecamp is perhaps the most well known of the bunch. It's designed to be fast loading and simple to use, and the clean, clutter-free interface is held in high regard by many. Keep in mind though that the simplicity and ease of use comes at a price: Basecamp doesn't have as many features as some of the more advanced project management systems.

To-do List: Wunderlist (earndifferent.com/wunderlist)

There might actually be even more to-do list services than project management services out there. It's a popular service to build apparently, most likely because it's a deceptively simple idea. It's not easy to get it exactly right though, and there are many poor implementations out there. Wunderlist is one of the best, with pleasing aesthetics and all the functionality you could ask for. It's also free to use, and multiplatform so you can use it on all your devices.

(Bonus tip: Some people actually find it better to use a plain old pen & paper for to-do lists. If you've tried software and online services but can't seem to stick with any of them, give the old-fashioned method a go!)

Time Tracking: Toggl (earndifferent.com/toggl)

Whatever your profession is, you may sooner or later find yourself requiring time tracking of some kind. Some project management tools have it built-in, but if you prefer a light-weight, standalone alternative you should check out Toggl. It doesn't get any easier to use, and in many situations it's completely free to use.

Time Management: RescueTime

(earndifferent.com/rescuetime)

If you find yourself easily distracted while working, or just want to see how you *really* spend all those hours in front of the computer, check out RescueTime. It lets you track everything you do on your computer, and create reports showing exactly how you spend your time. This can be a real wake-up call!

Block Unproductive Websites: LeechBlock

(earndifferent.com/leechblock)

LeechBlock is a browser add-on for Chrome and Firefox that lets you block time-wasting websites during working hours. If you regularly find yourself wasting time on Facebook and Youtube when you really should be working, installing a tool like that can really help you become more productive. Keep in mind though that you will need at least *some* willpower to ensure you don't just disable it when you feel your Facebook addiction calling!

Note Taking/Management: Evernote

(earndifferent.com/evernote)

If your computer is overflowing with notes and documents that "could be useful someday", you may want to check out Evernote. It lets you store all the little bits and pieces of information you collect throughout your day in an easily searched repository. You'll have everything in the same place, accessible from all your devices. This is especially useful for information hoarders, but most of us are probably guilty of not organizing our documents in the best way.

Dictation: Dragon NaturallySpeaking

(earndifferent.com/dragon)

For those who spend much of their day typing, it may be worth checking out Dragon NaturallySpeaking.

Many people find dictating much faster and easier than typing things out, meaning productivity will increase with a tool like this. It's also great if you're suffering from carpal tunnel syndrome or anything else that prevents you from working long hours on a keyboard. It may not be the best choice if you're not a native English speaker though, as it requires good pronunciation to work as intended.

Accounting/Invoicing: Quickbooks

(earndifferent.com/quickbooks)

Financial software is rarely easy to use, but Quickbooks is a notable exception. It's perhaps the most popular solution for simple accounting and invoicing today, and it's quite affordable too. Unless your business has very specific requirements and need an advanced accounting solution, Quickbooks will most likely be more than enough.

Password Management: LastPass

(earndifferent.com/lastpass)

You probably already know that you should have a unique password on every website you have an account with. The question is, how on earth are you supposed to keep track of all these passwords? Easy! Use a password manager like LastPass. With a tool like this, all your passwords will be stored in an encrypted database accessible through one single master password. It's very convenient, secure and it works on most platforms. If you prefer a non-commercial solution and hosting your password database yourself, check out KeePass which is a decent alternative.

Monitor Adjustment: f.lux (earndifferent.com/flux)

Let's face it: our bodies aren't really designed to spend all day in front of a computer, and that includes our eyes. This tool quietly adjusts your monitor color temperature throughout the day to match your surroundings. During the day your monitor will match the natural sunlight, and when evening comes around it will match your indoor lights. This is, in many cases, a love-or-hate app. Some people swear by it, while others find it highly irritating. Give it a try and see what you think, especially if your eyes get tired or you find it hard to sleep after a long day at work.

Takeaways

- *There are many helpful tools out there but you don't need to use all of them; use those that make sense for your own situation*
- *For almost every tool in the list there are a number of alternatives, so if you don't like the software suggested a simple Google search can more often than not reveal other suggestions to try*
- *While software can increase your productivity, it can never replace a good work ethic, so don't expect miracles from it*

Pro Tips

Keep a routine and schedule breaks

When you first start working from home, keeping a routine may be the last thing you want to do. After being forced to show up at work day after day at the exact same time, possibly for years, you probably can't wait to take the days as they come. The problem is that a lack of routines is usually not good for productivity, and if you want to ensure you really get things done, it's usually best to work around the same times every day.

Some people work best in the mornings, others are night owls who can't even spell their name before 10 am. You may have to do some experimenting when you're starting out to find a schedule/routine that works for you, and has you the most productive throughout the day.

Don't forget to take breaks regularly either, at least once per hour. It's easy to forget when you get into a good flow and the world around you fades away, so you may have to use a timer to remind you. Take 5 or 10 minutes to get up from the computer and maybe do some light stretching.

Many people who work from home swear by the "Pomodoro" technique. The idea is to separate your work into shorter intervals, usually 25 minutes, and take a 5 minute break after each interval. After four repetitions you take a longer break (15-30 minutes).

Some feel this technique leaves them energized and focused working throughout the day. Others find it annoying to be "forced" to take breaks when they may just have gotten into a good flow. Try it and see if it works for you!

Plan your work

Even if keeping a routine has you in your office at regular times, ready to work, you also need to plan your workday so you're making the most of it. For most people keeping a simple to-do list does the trick. The last thing you'll do every day before getting off work is writing the to-do list for the next day. This way you'll always be in control of your work, and you'll never have to wonder what to do next.

Get out of the house

Let's face it: working from home can get lonely, especially if you live alone. In order not to feel completely isolated, it can be helpful to try to schedule some time out of the house at least a few times per week. Some people even go as far as working out of a coffee shop once in a while; as long as you buy something the staff usually won't mind, and most of the time they offer free wi-fi access too.

If you prefer keeping your actual work at home, how about scheduling a lunch with a friend once per week? A simple "event" like that can be enough to stave off the feelings of isolation and break monotony.

Some people go as far as inventing little daily routines that get them out of the house. It doesn't have to be anything fancy or complicated, something simple like just taking a short drive to pick up some coffee every morning can work just fine. The important thing is you get some change of scenery.

Establish boundaries

One problem with working from home is that some family, friends and relatives might interpret your "flexible schedule" as "free to help them with whatever they need, whenever they need it". If you're not careful with this and learn to say no, you're going to find yourself stressed out trying to accommodate everyone and still have time for work.

Of course it's OK to take a few hours off now and then to help a friend or family member in need, but make sure you communicate clearly that taking time off is really what you're doing - no different from someone working a regular job.

Consider putting on work clothes

This is a technique some people swear by, while others find it completely unnecessary, even counterproductive. The idea is to make the distinction between work and leisure time even clearer by showering in the morning and dressing as if going to an actual office. This also helps communicate to others that you are actually working and not just lazing around the house. Some people, however, find that wearing comfortable (but not necessarily professional) clothes is much better for their productivity. Try both alternatives and see what you like best!

Invest in your office (and keep it tidy)

Don't expect to be at your most productive if you're not happy with your home office. You're most likely going to spend at least 8 hours in your office every day, and the closer it resembles your idea of a "dream office", the more fun it will be going to work every day.

You don't have to go overboard and invest thousands into fancy decor and expensive equipment if you don't want to, but a few simple touches such as a comfy couch and some nice art can go a long way. Don't be afraid to add some personal touches either - it doesn't have to look anything like a strict, regular workplace if you don't want it to!

It also helps productivity greatly to try to keep your home office tidy and clutter free, helping your mind focus on your actual work instead of your messy surroundings.

Take care of yourself

Regardless of where you work, you need to keep your body in decent shape to stay productive. This is another area where having a routine really helps. For most people hitting the gym once or twice per week, combined with a walk now and then when the weather allows, is more than enough. You could also buy some equipment and build a home gym, but then you'd be missing out on the 'out of the house' factor which, as you've seen, is a good thing to have.

Even if you go for walks and hit the gym regularly, you may still find yourself with an aching body after a long day in front of the computer. If that's the case, you may want to look into some stretching routines you can do every day to minimize the discomfort. Also make sure your workspace is setup properly from an ergonomic standpoint - as discussed earlier it pays off in the long run to spend a few extra bucks on a good chair and desk. There are plenty of videos on YouTube showing how you should set it all up to be as ergonomic as possible.

Many people who work from home find themselves either overeating (since the kitchen is likely just a few steps away), or not eating enough (because they get in "the zone" and simply forget about it when there's no one there to remind them). Don't make these mistakes! Just as you should keep your workday on a fixed schedule for best results, you should also schedule your meals. Everyone is different so you'll have to make your own plan here, but the focus should be on not letting yourself get *too* hungry, as your work will then most likely suffer as your blood sugar levels drop.

Keeping some healthy snacks available at all times can be very helpful, as can cooking all your meals for the whole week on the weekend and microwaving your lunches. This saves a lot of time and minimizes the risk of you choosing something unhealthy for lunch, like picking up fast food.

Eliminate distractions

While a rare few people might be able to watch TV while they're working and still stay productive, most of us cannot. In fact, even if the TV isn't in the same room it can still be distracting enough to hamper productivity if the volume is loud, and if you don't live alone you may have to either shut the door around you when you're working, or ask your spouse or roommates to keep it down so you can focus.

The same goes for all other noisy activities that can take place in your home, such as vacuuming or playing with children/pets. If you know you're easily distracted by such noises, you may want to consider placing your home office in a room as far away as possible from where these activities usually take place. Also, make sure the people you live with understand fully that you are working, and if you shut the door it doesn't mean you're angry with them, just that you need to concentrate.

If you get a lot of phone calls or texts during the day you may also want to set your phone to silent mode while you're working (unless you expect calls from clients/customers). Nothing is worse for productivity than being constantly bombarded with things that that require your immediate attention.

Social media

Another common and often problematic distraction is social media. Whether it's Twitter, Facebook or Reddit you're spending time on, chances are you aren't making any money while you're doing it, hence you should limit it to when you're not working. It's very easy to kill several hours per day on social networks, and that's something you cannot afford when you're trying to get some work done.

However, if you use social media in a professional capacity, you may just have to work it into your schedule. A good option might be checking it at the beginning and end of your day, and possibly also around lunchtime.

Do your chores and errands outside work hours

This is somewhat related to keeping a routine/schedule. When you work from home you will most likely sooner or later notice housework that needs taking care of. It could be taking out the trash or washing the dirty dishes piling up in the sink. The problem is, if you start doing one of these chores you may end up wasting hours of your workday. Just like everything else that's not directly work related, it should be limited to before or after work if you want to ensure maximum productivity.

Leave work at the end of the day

When you're working from home it can be difficult to let go when you're done working for the day. After all, your office is right there, you could just pop in and take care of some e-mails, right?

Sure, there might not be much harm in doing this once in a while, but you also need to learn to separate your work and private life, or else you might risk burning yourself out. Most people who haven't tried it think of working from home as relaxing and somewhat carefree, but the truth is it can become the complete opposite if you let it. You may even have to turn off your computer and shut the door to your office at the end of the day to eliminate this problem, otherwise the temptation may be too great.

Don't forget to have fun!

While work and staying productive is important, it's certainly not everything, and your whole life shouldn't revolve around it. Even if you have a pressing deadline coming up this week, don't forget to set aside some time after work to have fun and relax. Yes, sometimes you'll simply have to go into "crunch mode" and work as hard as you can, but if you keep that up for too long you'll burn out fast.

Develop your own strategy

Even if all these suggestions we've gone over will work for most people, it's important to remember that everyone is different and there is no right or wrong here. If avoiding routines and schedules completely does in fact make you more productive, or you feel the increase in mental well-being is worth the sacrifice in productivity, go for it! One of the best things about working from home is that no one can tell you what to do.

Takeaways

- *Most people who work from home find it beneficial to keep to a set schedule, plan their days carefully and develop daily routines*
- *It's very important to clearly separate work from non-work, doing chores and hobbies outside work hours*
- *If you aren't careful it's very easy to become distracted by things happening in the house, TV or social media*
- *While work is important, don't forget to disconnect once in a while and just have some fun!*
- *Even though some tips and advice should work for most people, you should still experiment and find your own optimal strategy*

Part 2:

Your 10 Step Plan

Step 1: Plan Your Knowledge

For you to have the courage and desire in you to succeed as an entrepreneur is a unique and exciting thing. Not many people have the guts to leave the corporate world and make something of themselves on their own – much less online.

That may be because it's a viable business opportunity that very few people understand. They know there are websites online and they see people making money, but they have no idea how to get from step A to step B.

Fear often keeps us rooted to a career that we can't stand.

It doesn't matter what your reasons are for pursuing this path. Maybe you are out of work and looking for a job in an economy that has none to offer. Perhaps you're a stay at home parent who would like to contribute to the household finances. Or maybe you're retired but just not yet ready to quit being productive!

One thing is for sure. That old saying, "If you fail to plan, plan to fail" is true.

So that's what you're going to start with – the planning elements that go into building a business like this.

Shiny New Object Syndrome

The shiny new object syndrome is a beast that chases all new work at home entrepreneurs. It feeds off of your desire to be making money FAST and EASY and it's a drug you don't want to become addicted to.

You may start off with this very book that you're reading now – and then later today someone in a forum mentions that they made $1,019 in just 24 hours with XYZ info product.

Before you know it, the shiny new object syndrome has taken root and you've whipped out your credit card and ordered it – instantly becoming that much more in debt before ever implementing a single step from this guide.

You're not alone if you've succumbed to this disease of mindset.

But you have to nip it in the bud before it gets out of control. In most cases, the people suffering from this affliction don't take action on a regular basis. They simply buy, read, analyze and buy the next shiny new object that gets in their line of sight.

You're going to be bombarded with new things that make your mouth water or your wallet itch. They will come from a myriad of places, such as:

- *Forum posts where people you're learning right alongside with rave about new products coming out.*

- *Email autoresponders from those you've signed up with – maybe for a freebie.*

- *Ads you see in sidebars on someone's blog.*

- *Reviews you read from seemingly honest marketers.*

- *Google results as you go online to search for information about making money online.*

- *Word of mouth as you befriend others on the same journey.*

There are just a few problems with the recommendations I listed above.

With forums, you need to know that not all posts are created equal. Unfortunately, there's a lot of the "buddy system" roaming around online. This is when a group of friends agrees to post for one another whenever they launch a new product.

They call it a "mastermind group." Not all mastermind groups are like this, but some are. So let's say Bob has a new product about List Building. One of the people in his group, we'll call him Joe, goes into a forum and posts a question such as, "Does anyone know where I can get a good list building product?"

Then the rest of the group goes in to post that they're using Bob's new product and it's absolutely amazing!

What happens is YOU see a huge list of people who are excited about this product. The sad thing is, it's just a "you scratch my back, I'll scratch yours" situation.

Are ALL posts like this shady and unseemly? Of course not! But how will you know? Protect your wallet and let the reviews simmer for awhile. If general feedback in multiple places is that it's good, then maybe give it a try.

You don't want to be chasing the trendy, "about to be banned" tactics anyway, so don't be in a rush to grab something that won't be a fairly evergreen strategy for you to implement.

With email autoresponders, you're lured into a list with an amazing freebie. Maybe you bought the person's product and it was fantastic. Unfortunately, what many marketers do to make money online is called "list swapping."

This means they'll promise to promote someone else's product if the other person promises to promote for them. So Bob might agree to promote Joe's product if Joe promotes to his list.

You're on Bob's list, so you get an email from him touting the benefits of Joe's product. This may not even be anything Bob believes in, but he's holding up his end of the list swapping agreement.

Unless the marketer admits he hasn't read it, or shows you some information about how he himself implemented it, be wary of an email like this.

With ads that you see in sidebars, you have to be careful. You might trust a marketer and see an ad that recommends a new product. You go and buy it and it's pure trash.

It could be just an AdSense ad that the blogger or site owner doesn't personally endorse. If you're wondering about it, always contact the site owner and ask if they are personally promoting the product or if it's just an AdSense ad.

Sometimes you're going to encounter a review for a product. You see it being promoted so you type into

Google, "XYZ product name review." A whole list of entries pops up and you read them – they're all glowing testimonials about the benefits of the product.

That doesn't mean it's true. Some people are so desperate to make money online that they give a positive review to anything that's released – especially items where they'll make a nice 50% commission.

Look for signs that the reviewer actually implemented the product. Is the review simply stating facts that can be found on the sales page? If so, it probably means they haven't personally looked it over.

Now Google results can be tricky to new entrepreneurs. Let's say you go online and type in "make money online" to the Google search engine. You may think that the first several results would be the most beneficial, since their sites are ranked first in the search engine.

But if you look closely on the upper right corner, you'll see a tiny word that says, "Ads." These people are paying for that position. And you can't rely on search engine results pages (SERPs) to give you the best information anyway. Too many marketers know how to play by the SEO rules and get their sites ranked high, even if they provide no real value.

Lastly, you're going to hear about products through word of mouth. If you have a friend online who you trust completely, then by all means go ahead and take their advice.

But if you're at a seminar and there's a buzz going around about a new guru's product, be careful that you're not just listening to a bunch of people kissing up to someone who has gained a bit of celebrity in this small circle.

Information Overload

Even with one single product on your hard drive, you can easily begin to feel overwhelmed with information overload. If this happens to you, realize that it's not uncommon and it is beatable!

Information overload generally happens in one of two situations:

1.) You bought too many products and you're trying to do them all at once.

If you bought too many products, it's okay – let's just clean things up from here. I want you to choose ONE to work from right now. You can't go with everything all at once. Implementation has to be progressive.

You *build* this business – it doesn't just all appear at once. This guide will give you a good idea of what order you should go in with branding, list building, affiliate marketing, info product creation, etc.

And don't try to do more in a day that you really can. You're going to suffer burnout if you overload yourself with information and tasks. At the same time, if you want to move forward, you have to start taking action steps seriously.

2.) You only have one product, but you're letting fear and frustration get in the way of your success.

This second dilemma is troublesome because it's hard to gain confidence in yourself when you have nothing to go by. You have no prior success (and maybe even quite a few failures) with your online income efforts.

The first thing you want to do is set aside a certain amount of time to work each day on implementing a guide (even this one). You can break it up if it's more convenient for you, but don't try working from sun up to sun down and end up in tears because you're exhausted.

As you implement a course, do it section by section in the order that the product creator has given. Don't jump around. And don't skip steps because you don't want to do them.

One common problem is that product owners generalize an instruction without giving you details. This can be very frustrating, but stay calm! The first thing you want to do is Google it!

For example, let's say a guide tells you to "post your YouTube video on your blog." Well they don't tell you HOW! You have no clue. Go to Google and type in that exact question: "how to post a YouTube video on your blog."

You'll get a ton of step-by-step results. Now a good idea would be to email the product owner at the end of your implementation and let them know what steps you had to seek elsewhere so they can make it better for the next buyer, but this is not your responsibility – just a courtesy to make the web a better place.

Take the course in bite sized steps. Don't try to implement an entire course in two hours. If you succeed, it'll be sloppy. And you won't retain much of the information, either.

If you do run into a roadblock where the answers can't be found on Google, then try asking in a marketing forum. Feel free to contact the product owner, too. They should have some support for the product and if you run into a stone wall with no reply and no answers, then it's acceptable to ask for a refund at this point.

Scams

Scams are prevalent online and it's one reason the FTC is cracking down on false claims and going after marketers who abuse people. You're going to encounter them – to what level varies.

You might encounter someone selling a product that's good, but you lose trust in the product creator. This might be someone selling a "make money online" product and you see them posting in a forum that their truck broke down and they're trying to get free handouts to fix it. Makes you scratch your head and say, "Hmmmm."

Or you may find someone promoting a product that turns out to be black hat. Black hat is often viewed as unethical and sometimes it's illegal. It's basically a way to game the system in a less than honest manner.

The worst types of scams are those where the promoter takes your money and never delivers. You do have protection, but you have to know where to find it. First, try getting a refund from the shopping cart method – PayPal or ClickBank (earndifferent.com/clickbank) for example.

If that doesn't work and the promoter isn't responding to your emails, don't be shy about taking serious action. Simply go to the FBI's Internet Fraud Complaint Center (earndifferent.com/fbi) and initiate an investigation. You can also let the product owner know that you've done this so that even if the FBI doesn't take on your complaint, it will probably scare the promoter into refunding you fairly quickly.

Who Can You Trust?

All of this negative talk might make you scared to go forward but I have some good news. There are a LOT of ethical, moral individuals out there teaching fellow entrepreneurs how to succeed.

You're going to have to find out who delivers on their promises and who drops the ball. Ask around in forums. Sign up to several lists and sit back and analyze and watch the marketer's emails.

Ask yourself some questions as you size up a marketer you're considering learning from:

- *Are they doing nothing but pushing product to you on a daily basis?*

- *Do they promote products that have earned poor reviews from many others?*

- *Do they answer emails from you?*

- *Are they transparent in what you're doing online?*

- *Do they give value to you free as much as they push paid products on you?*

If you ever see red warning flags, simply remove them from your "trustworthy" list and move on. Don't just go off of what others say, although it's a good place to start. Remember what I said about the buddy system – you never know who's promoting or giving positive feedback about someone *just* because they're a friend.

Step 2: Plan Your Mindset

You might be rolling your eyes thinking mindset isn't an issue, but you'd be surprised. It can cripple you before you even start becoming financially successful online.

There's No Room for Desperation

Many people reading this are here because they're desperate for money. It's a trap that can cause you to make poor business decisions and it may even put you further in debt.

People are desperate for money for a variety of reasons:

- *They just got laid off and can't find a job.*
- *They're employed fulltime, but unable to make ends meet.*
- *They make ends meet but have zero money left over for luxuries.*
- *They're retired but their income doesn't afford them the lifestyle they want.*
- *They want to be a contributing member of the household.*

If you're unemployed and desperate for money, it might be faster to take a job below your normal income offline to take the pressure off with bill collectors. Building an online business takes time.

That doesn't mean you can't start earning right away, but consider these details:

- *If you're an affiliate for a site like Amazon, you're going to be waiting 60 days to get paid for today's earnings.*

- *If you get hired for a long-term project like the creation of an eBook, for example, the funds will sit in escrow while you do the work and you won't get the money until it's delivered.*

- *If you're selling digital products, you may have to wait for the site to pick up in traffic before you start making significant sales.*

You may only be able to work on your online business part time, and that's okay! But it'll take a bit longer to see formidable earnings.

Desperation is a cancer on your business growth, so don't give in to it. If you need to, get an offline job to cover the bills and take baby steps as you grow this online business into something that eventually takes over your need to be employed elsewhere.

Test the Waters Before You Commit

Keeping desperation at bay, you want to take time to evaluate which business model you want to pursue. This book is going to cover the main ones (and there are micro models too).

You want to look at each one to see where you wish to begin. But I want you to keep this in mind: you never want all your eggs in one basket.

You're going to choose one model to build the foundation with and then add the others to your online marketing strategy. For example, you might:

- *Start with the offer of ghostwriting services.*

- *Add an info product of your own.*

- *Begin promoting other people's products as an affiliate.*

- *Include some ads and start collecting revenue.*

Do some online searches and learn as much as you can for free about the various ways to make money online. Do this before you pay money for any products.

If you see that a system just isn't for you – meaning it's not personally satisfying and you're dreading working on it each day, then drop it and move on to something that you enjoy.

After all, why choose a work at home career if you're not in charge of your destination? This should be profitable, but it should also be enjoyable!

Fail Your Way to Success

Did you start an affiliate site and not make any sales? Launch a product and no one bought it? Don't give up! Just find out the reasons why your business model didn't perform and tweak them for success.

The great thing about working at home online is that your content and strategies can be altered quickly and you're continually learning new things.

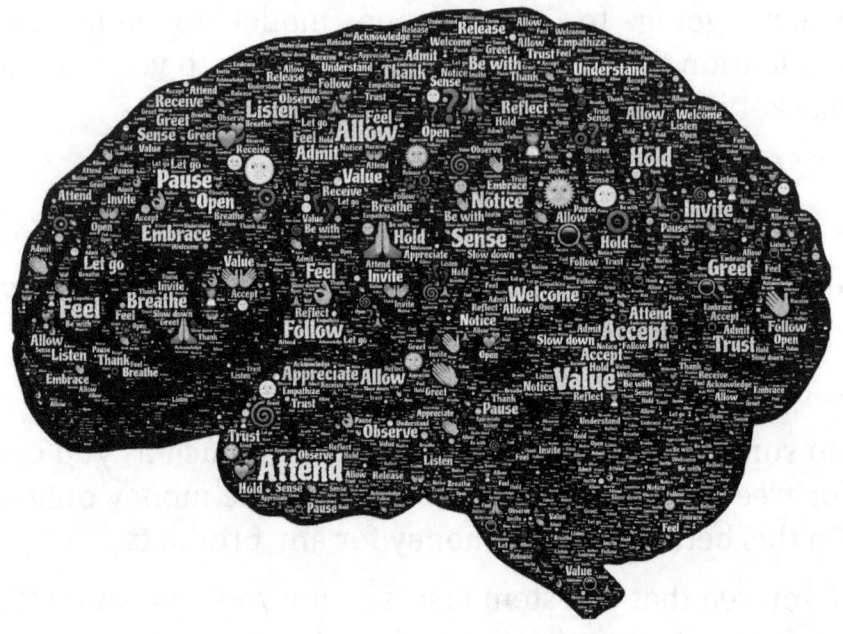

Step 3: Prepare Your Family

When you first tell friends and family that you're going to pursue a work at home career, be prepared for some less than enthusiastic responses. This is normal and understandable so try not to get defensive about it.

The key is to learn how to best handle their reactions and assuage their fears. You're going to have to plan your business out a little so that you can present them with the facts and let them see that you're serious and you know what you're doing.

Show Them You Mean Business

The first step is in showing your family that this is a viable business opportunity. They're going to have heard about online money scams. Reassure them that you're not talking about pyramid schemes or other types of scams.

By the time you're finished with this boo, you should have a basic blueprint for your business. Before you even approach your spouse or parents (or kids) with this idea, try to map out what you plan to do in a semblance of steps.

Print out a copy for each family member to peruse.

Remember – they may be worried that you're not going to make money, that you're going to get scammed, or that you're not going to be available for them anymore.

Make a FAQ page for them, and answer questions like these:

- *What will my new schedule be like?*
- *Will I still be available for activities like taking you to ballet class?*
- *Am I going to shut myself off in a home office?*
- *Are we going to lose our house, get the phone cut off, etc.?*
- *How much money am I going to spend starting up this business?*

Ask them for feedback. If they have any additional questions, write them down and answer them for them once you've had a little while to mull it over in your mind.

Never roll your eyes or belittle their concerns. You want their support during this journey, so it's important that you make them feel like their input is valuable to you.

Answering The Common Question, "What Do You Do?"

This is a tough question and it begins once you're no long getting up and dressed to fight traffic on the way to a J-O-B. People are going to look at you like you're an alien – everyone from the postal delivery person to the cashier who sees you grocery shopping at 10 AM.

In-laws and your own parents and siblings might ask, "But I don't understand – what is it you *DO*?"

There's no way on earth that you can explain Internet Marketing in a quick 15-minute casual conversation.

They're going to assume you're a spammer because they've always received spam emails to their inbox advertising "work at home" money or some sort of pills that work wonders.

Reassure them that you're not a spammer.

They may assume you're in the adult industry – running one of "those kinds" of sites. Let them know it's nothing of the sort.

Others may ask if you're stuffing envelopes because they've seen magazine ads for that type of business in the backs of their favorite magazines.

Here's something you can tell to the people who ask what you do as a "work at home" entrepreneur:

"I have several streams of income that I'm developing that all tie in together. One is the creation of informative eBooks, like the kind you see people reading on their Kindles. I teach people how to _____ (train their dogs, lose weight). I also operate a blog and review products for people to see if they're worth investing money in. Sometimes I _____(service: ghostwrite, build websites) for other people. And my sites also bring in some money with ads that are on the side."

Throwing in the Kindle brand name helps bring some "Ah yes, I've seen that" recognition and legitimacy.

Most people have heard of – and even admire – bloggers. This is a good way to explain your affiliate marketing and lets them view you as a helpful consumer advocate rather than a spammy marketer.

Balancing Work and Home Life

Just because work is in the home doesn't mean that you don't need a slight separation of the two. To some people, trying to work amid the TV, kids screaming, and other distractions is a recipe for disaster.

Others can easily tune it out and get a lot of work down, while surrounded by their loving family members and they actually enjoy the continual interaction they have amid getting work done.

You want to make sure that you have a good balance between the two. Don't work so much that you're home, but never "there" for your family. It's tempting to get on a run and work for 16 hours straight – it's rewarding when it's your own business that you're pushing for.

It's also easy to fall into the trap of lazing around the house when you work for yourself. After all, there's no boss to answer to – no clients sitting across from you.

If your family sees you pulling this stunt, they're going to lose faith in you quickly. You want them to see a productive worker – but that doesn't necessarily mean a typical 8-5 schedule.

There's nothing in the rulebook that says you have to wake up at 6 and start work at 8. You can set your own hours, as long as you have some hours to put in. You may be able to spend a lot more time with your family, putting their needs first for several hours, and sit down to focus on your work needs later in the day when everyone's settled in.

This can be very rewarding to everyone involved. Just don't let the scales tip so that one element of your life begins to overshadow the other. Keep track of your hours initially until you feel comfortable with your routine.

Don't be afraid to change things up if you need to. For instance, if your usual schedule is to work from 10 AM to 3 PM, but your child is sick and you need to take him to the doctor, then rearrange your schedule to accommodate the care taking you need to work in for the day.

After all, what's the use of working for yourself and not having to call in and ask for permission if you aren't going to be flexible with *yourself*?

Setting Up a Work Space – Or Not

Creating workspace for your work at home career can vary from no space to offsite space – and everything in between, of course. It has to fit your personal working style and you may need to be immersed in working for yourself before you truly know what you'll prefer.

Some people need nothing more than a laptop and connection to the Internet. They may sit in their favorite recliner or even wake up in bed and grab their laptop to work from.

Others rent out a space away from their home to work in. This requires a pretty substantial investment of money in the beginning, but if you have it and feel you need the separation from home, then it can help your productivity.

Many people assign a certain room of their homes to be office space. It doesn't even have to be an entire room – it can be a corner of the room. You'll need to determine what you need in the way of space.

Do you have an entire desk to work at? Or is a laptop holder plenty for you? Are you working with a normal sized desktop PC? You can get very small desks that don't take up much room.

Some people like to have the following elements for their home office:

- *A computer (some marketers wind up with multiple computers)*
- *A webcam*
- *Speakers*
- *Portable video device such as Flip or Kodak with tripod*
- *Back up storage hard drive (don't lose your hard work!)*
- *Phone and fax (these are not necessary but some like to have it anyway)*

Some things you want to do are make sure you're not allowing distractions to keep you from being productive. Having the TV on might not affect you – or you could get so engrossed in the latest Headline News court trial that you're glued to the TV more than your own business!

Making Sure You Don't Neglect Your Duties

We all have responsibilities in life. We have a responsibility to keep our homes tidy, to take care of ourselves, to nurture our children, and to prosper financially so that we're supporting our own families.

You have to make sure that you're organized enough to recognize if anything's not getting the love and attention it deserves – and that goes for your business just like your own offspring.

Make a list of personal and business tasks that you'd like to get done each day. Don't beat yourself up if you were overzealous in brainstorming and didn't get to cross off half of what you wrote down.

Just adjust for the next day so that you'll know how much you can feasibly get done in a 24-hour timespan. You may find that you've even underestimated yourself.

WAH Doesn't Mean Available 24/7

Here's something very annoying that's bound to happen to you:

You're getting up and readying yourself for a productive work day and someone – a spouse, a neighbor, a good friend – calls and asks you to do an errand for them.

Many people assume that because you have no boss to answer to, that it's okay to ask you to be at *their* beck and call.

You need to put a stop to this before it gets out of control. If you immediately respond with, "Oh, I'm so sorry – I'm working on a big project right now," it will show them that they can't assume you'll be their errand boy (or girl).

If you start doing favors all around town for everyone, it will start a chain reaction that has everyone calling on you when they need you to pick up their kids or take their dry cleaning in for them or drop off their lunch that they forgot to bring to the office.

As an entrepreneur, the best thing you can do for your business is take it seriously. If you're always doing things for others, then you won't be building anything solid   for   yourself.

Step 4: Plan Your Branding

We see it all the time with celebrities – branding that looks like a cute nickname, when it's really a whole lot more than that.

The Barefoot Contessa from the Food Network is a good example of branding. You instantly get the image of a beautiful Italian woman leisurely cooking a delicious homemade meal in the comfort of her own home.

30-Minute Meals is a brand that isn't instantly connected to a person's name, but immediately, you grasp the concept – simple and easy. This would appeal to very busy people.

Paula Deen used to be "The Lady and Sons" when she was starting out and had her sons as part of her main business. She became so popular that her name overshadowed her starting business brand.

Two Ways to Brand Your Business

You have a couple of options here. You can brand your business as a whole, or you can brand each site and endeavor individually. There are pros and cons to each.

It'd be nice to be the go to person for an umbrella niche – one that housed all of your efforts in one namesake. But if you're varying your business a little, it might be hard.

For example, a site that's on dog training and promotes tangible items on Amazon won't fit well with your Wedding Planning eBook.

It's okay to have multiple brands. You might be the "Dog Training Aid Advisor" or the "Wedding Wonder Woman" – but you can brand each site on its own.

If you feel uncomfortable about using your real name for a lot of different things, then use pen names that you make up for the rest. Or brand it as a business entity with an angle, not a name, such as:

- *Weddings Under $5,000*
- *Fat Free Fare*
- *Paintball Pro Guide*

...you get the idea.

But I'm Not an Expert!

Some entrepreneurs (especially those new to online marketing) get very anxious about being an expert – or I should say, *not* being an expert.

You don't have to worry so much about your authority and expertise. You're going to tout it without having to be perfect. There's no PhD required. No college education required.

Now this might be more difficult to achieve in certain niches. For instance, if you start trying to dispense serious medical advice on your website, you might have some trouble with people wanting to verify your credentials.

But what expertise would you need to have with the weigh loss niche, for example? You could enter into this niche without ever having had a weight problem. Teach good, solid advice that's not going to endanger anyone and you'll be fine.

Or, if you were once overweight and now have used certain methods to slim down, share those with others and your own journey makes you an expert of sorts.

Don't try deceiving your customers. This isn't worth it – and with the FTC cracking down on scams, you don't want to get caught having made false claims that could get you into trouble.

Branding Through Social Networks

Social networking can be promising if you use it the right way. The problem is, many marketers teach unethical branding methods and then you risk getting banned or creating a bad reputation for yourself as a spammer.

Interactive social networking sites, where you're watching a stream of posts and commenting and sharing are sites like:

- Twitter (earndifferent.com/twitter)
- Facebook (earndifferent.com/fb)
- Google+ (earndifferent.com/g+)

These sites all have certain restrictions for their terms of service, so you want to read those carefully. They may limit the number of links you can post, or keep tabs on which topics you write about.

Some have special branding tools available to you. For example, you can create a FaceBook fan page for your business. This is perfectly within their rules.

But if you go creating a profile for your page and start befriending and spamming people, you'll get shut down (and if they connect your *real* personal profile to it, they may nix both of them!

Google+ has said that everyone must use their real names, but they understand the importance of branding, too. So while the site is still in its infancy, they're working to create branding pages for those who want to market.

This is good because it keeps the marketing separate from the friendly interaction among users. Twitter is less strict about this type of communication, but they don't allow abuse of their network, either.

LinkedIn is a great place for you to join as a social media marketer. It can help you network with others in the same or relevant niches, but it's less about reaching your core audience.

Whenever you're using social media platforms for your networking and marketing efforts, try to share a variety of informational resources. You can share links, but don't only share your own.

If you're using forums as a platform for your marketing, then make sure you see if you're allowed to use a signature file, which is a way to hyperlink a short message or image to your own site each time you make a post or reply to someone else's.

On all of these sites, make sure that you brand your messages – with image and text recognition wherever possible. We'll get into that a bit more in just a minute. Whatever you do, complete your profile on the sites. An incomplete profile can hurt your branding abilities.

Branding Through an Image

An image can represent you online. It's great for your prospective customers to be able to put a face or logo to the name of your business. Here are some of the image opportunities you have to brand yourself online:

Avatars are the thumbnail images that are using in profiles on the web. If you comment on someone's blog, for example, then you may see your "gravatar" show up next to your comment.

Site graphics like a header, foot, and background can help brand your business online. You can order ordinary templates that brand your niche to some degree, but they won't be customized to help you build a specific brand name.

Video can even carry your brand image in it. You can create or order an introduction and ending to insert into your videos. It could be a combination of music with your logo and a tag line to introduce your video content.

Don't try to use images that you create yourself if they appear unprofessional. This is a business, so you want your brand to shine through – even on a thumbnail!

You have options for ordering custom made branding images. You can go to someone who specializes in that particular media format. For instance, there are minisite designers who can create a "per site" brand for you for about $100 – which includes:

- *Header*
- *Footer*
- *Background*
- *Testimonial box*
- *Opt in box*
- *Order buttons*

If you prefer to have designers come to you, then consider placing a project on a site like Upwork (earndifferent.com/upwork) where people can bid on your project and you can browse portfolios.

If you're using your own picture as an avatar or other image, consider what type of image you want to project. You may even want to get a professional to photograph you.

Branding Through Text

Branding also comes in the form of the content that you post online. You should always be thinking about what you want your brand to project. Unless your intention is controversy, try to watch what you say under your brand's profiles.

Regardless of what your niche is, you want to project authority and expertise in your niche – even if you're new to it! There's nothing wrong with being honest and saying:

- *"I'm going to conduct a review of _____ and tell you what my thoughts are!" [affiliate marketing]*

- *"I was tired of not being able to find good information on _____, so I scoured everything and compiled the best data I could find on _____ so that you don't have to!" [info product creation]*

- *"I'm just starting out ghostwriting online, but my passion for non fiction writing surpasses my client list right now – which means my schedule is open for YOU!" [services]*

Keep track of any and all publicity that your brand receives and toot your own horn about it. If someone on another blog writes something positive about you, then talk about it and link to their blog so they can see the kudos for themselves.

Make sure you have an easy contact format for people to get ahold of you to discuss your brand. This could result in interviews on many formats – radio, TV, and other online sites.

Complete your "About" page on your site. Some people neglect this or simply give a short paragraph on what the company is, but a good About page goes into detail about the brand and what its goals are.

Set up a Google Alert (earndifferent.com/alert) so that you can get instant notification of whenever someone posts about your name or your brand name. This way if there's a fire, you can put it out and if it's something positive, you can help create a buzz about it. Implement these ideas, too:

- *Offer to guest blog on other people's sites.*

- *Put out a newsletter that has tips, emphasizing your expertise.*

Personal branding for your name or a business entity can help further your online profits – much more than if you leave it to fate to make *your* site the one a consumer happens to buy from.

Step 5: Plan Your List Building

Over and over again, you're going to hear, "The gold is in the list!" You hear that and instantly get worried because you don't HAVE a list. Well that's an easy thing to fix.

The problem starts when people don't build their list the right way, or they abuse their list just to tap into that "gold" and watch as it dwindles down and dries up because you let word get around that you're nothing but a product pusher.

So we're going to go over five things you need to know about list building, and we'll start with how you view this whole opportunity of communication with your customers and prospects.

Nailing Down Your Purpose

Are you seeing dollar signs because you're envious of the top marketers who have 100,000 people on their lists? Let me be frank with you – size of your list isn't what determines your profits.

Many of the top marketers in terms of list size perform very poorly on conversions when they blast a promotion to their list. Why do you think this is? It isn't because the offer isn't any good in some cases.

What happens is, marketers get greedy and do whatever they can to build up their list numbers, some even sharing names when they've previously promised not to!

And some, when trusted enough by a consumer to have their name and email address, see one form of success and decide to milk their list for all it's worth, turning from helpful guide to product pusher.

Your first step should be in knowing what the purpose of your list is – and it isn't to make money. That will come naturally. Your goal is twofold:

a.) Help people.

You're possibly in the mindset of helping yourself right now. That's understandable. But realize that it's personally rewarding to help others with whatever issues they may have – and word naturally spread, helping you make money in the process.

b.) Position yourself as an authority.

When you create value and help people, they tend to start regarding you as an expert in your field. You could be the first to even explain something that's been around awhile – in a way that many people prefer over what's already on the market!

Creating Automated Lesson Plans

There are two types of email autoresponders that will go out with your list building efforts – follow-ups and broadcasts. You want to fill your follow-up queue so that you're contacting the subscriber every 4th day or so.

This helps them maintain their recognition of you, it gives you more opportunities to brand yourself as a helpful authority figure, and it opens the door to them welcoming your occasional promotions, too.

You'll start with a simple welcome email to your list. This doesn't have to be anything earth shattering. If you've offered a freebie in your opt in box area, then make sure they have the download link to it here.

If you offered a series of emails, then go ahead and add those communications right away, so that they get what you promised to them. Never offer anything and start list building without having it in place already.

What happens if you promise a series of weekly email lessons and you get lazy and quit at week 12? Your prospect will feel let down and you'll lose points for the reputation you've been building with those initial contacts.

Emails don't have to be long. They can be half of a printed page (about 250 words) or longer, depending on whether or not you're promising to send a full newsletter.

You can find topics for your follow up emails just by using the free Google keyword tool (earndifferent.com/planner).Type in the broadest keyword for your niche. Let's use dog training as an example.

When I type in dog training, I get results that show me what a good series of follow up emails could be about, including:

- *Potty training*
- *Chewing issues*
- *Guard dogs*

Each email could be a unique lesson according to what has the most searches or whatever you find most interesting.

You can also use things like **Yahoo Answers** (earndifferent.com/answers) or **ChaCha** (earndifferent.com/chacha) to find topics to put in your email autoresponder, and forums provide good sleuthing opportunities to see what people in your niche want to know.

Knowing When to Push Promotions

You can promote inside your follow up emails or use the broadcast email system to blast out a one-time promotion. Or, use a combination of tactics. One good way to do it is this:

Use your follow-ups to promote evergreen items that you feel will be around for a long time. As the months and years pass, you don't want to have to revisit each follow up email to tweak it for what has recently fallen out of favor with your niche.

Whatever you do, ignore the advice to sell, sell, and sell some more!

Not every email needs to be a product push. Some marketers will tell you that you're leaving money on the table – that's okay. It's more important to focus on building brand loyalty because then you're able to sell to one person many times rather than trying to find a new person to sell to every single day (that's much harder!).

So when DO you promote products?

- *Whenever there's something timely you need to tell your subscribers about (like a special that ends in 48 hours, for example).*

- *Whenever you have a perk to offer them (like a special discount coupon they can use to buy something).*

- *Whenever you've finished reviewing a product and want to give your final stance on it.*

- *Whenever something new is released and they may not know about it.*

It's a good idea to listen to your subscribers and check their pulse on product promotions. If you start getting a bunch of unsubscribes, and they're telling you that all you do is promote, you might want to consider cutting back to see if your list retention improves.

Should You Go With Free or Paid Tools?

When you go into business, you're going to want to invest in certain things. One of them will be a list building tool. The messages that we discussed previously can all be done before you spend a penny.

However, know that there are limitations (not only in size of your list but sometimes topics that can be discussed) when using something free. Some free autoresponder tools might throw in ads that you don't want.

There are several paid yet very affordable (less than $20/month) email autoresponder tools like **AWeber** (earndifferent.com/aweber) that give you a free trial to see how you get on.

 Some companies will charge one flat monthly fee for using their service. Others may have a monthly charge that increases as your list grows. For example, you might have up to 10,000 people on your list for $20/month and then have to pay $50/month for the next 10,000 subscribers.

Long Term Growth for Your List

To keep building your list, you'll need to continue working on the traffic generation strategies we'll discuss later in this guide. Make sure you don't just send your traffic to a sales page but to a squeeze page (where your opt in box resides) first.

Once they're on your list, you'll be able to court them into having a viable marketing relationship with you. But if you send them to a sales page, they could be gone forever.

Why am I even discussing list building when you don't yet have a business model to pursue? It's because too many people fail right out of the gate by not starting to build their list on day 1.

They wait, and wait and wait – until suddenly they've been in the game for too long and don't realize that list building is the reason they're failing – they make one time sales on occasion but can't ever repeat the sale – and that's simply not enough to live on.

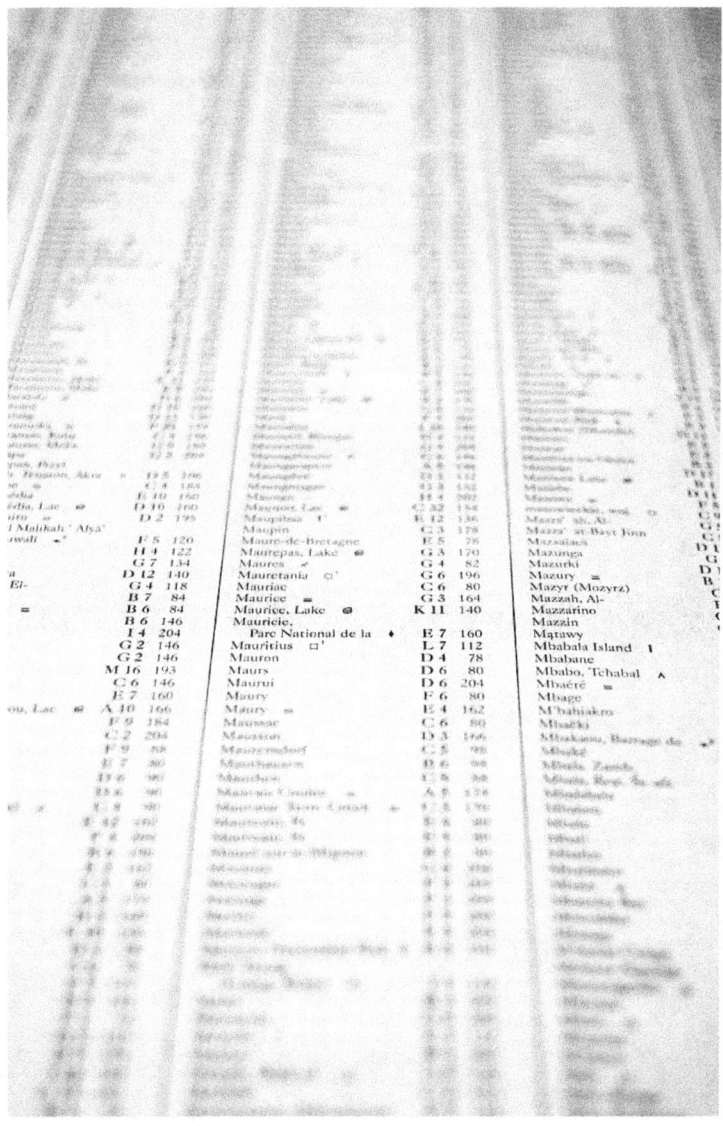

Step 6: Plan to Be of Service First

If your situation is one where money is a pressing matter (it's not always that way for some who just have an interest in working from home), then services are the fastest route to making money.

The premise of offering services is this:

You are not yet experienced and successful online. But there are MANY who are. And they range on levels of success – some make multi millions. Others make enough to survive on and are trying to grow their business but simply can't without a bit of extra help to free up some of their time.

So you step in to alleviate their time management woes. You're going to either be doing things they don't have time for – OR, taking over tasks they don't know HOW to do (like some people can't write).

I have some warnings for you with services that you need to heed:

- *They will feed off of your desperation – so keep it under wraps. If you post a bid on a project or approach a prospective client BEGGING for work, they'll get you to charge the very least amount possible, knowing you'll take it.*

- *You can't be afraid to stand up for yourself just because they know more than you about the online marketplace. For example – let's say you get hired to ghostwrite an eBook.*

You write it, but before you get paid, the marketer tells you that he doesn't want you to deliver it in Word or TXT but in HTML – so that his entire site is fully formatted for him and ready to upload.

This isn't a ghostwriting gig – it's writing paired with website creation! Tell him either "No, I only deliver the content," or, "Sure – but the website creation aspect will cost you an additional $___."

The sad thing is, some shady marketers actually teach others how to rip off service providers, so stand firm. It will NOT impact your earnings.

- *They ALL need their deliverables yesterday. Every marketer will try to rush you. This is because most service providers are notoriously late. So they feel like if they rush you, then maybe they'll get their stuff on time. Let them know a delivery date up front and if they can't accept that, let them find someone else.*

So now we're going to look at a few services that you can offer to fellow Internet marketers. You could have a site offering just one service, or mix and match a few offers.

If you want to, you can grow your own service business by bringing on a few other trusted service providers. You take in the money and keep a small percentage and then pay them the remainder.

Ghostwriting

This is the most predominant service marketers are after online. So many people can't write, or have no time to whip up content. They need content for many things, including:

- *Info products to sell (like eBooks)*
- *Blogs*
- *Website content*
- *Squeeze pages*
- *Email autoresponders*
- *Article directories*
- *Guest blog spots*
- *Viral reports (like free opt ins and sneak peek PDFs)*

And the great thing is, very few marketers only have one niche. So a single client could yield dozens upon dozens of projects for you in a wide variety of niche markets!

Now you may have some questions – like, "Is my writing good enough?" Writing online is a far different world than writing for a professor in college. It's conversational – look at this book you're reading now – could you write in an easy manner like this?

What can you earn ghostwriting? Well you might get scared off when you see a few people charging $4 per page. But most viable marketers don't hire these people – they feel there's a direct correlation between the price and the quality of the deliverables.

Most brand new ghostwriters start off charging about $7-10 per page (a page has about 430 words on it). You can raise your per page rates very quickly, but the key is to build yourself a reputation as a service provider who:

- *Writes unique content. So many writers simply rip off other people's content. Please don't do this – they can easily check it for uniqueness using free and paid tools online.*

- *Delivers good, quality writing. It doesn't have to be mind-blowing, but it should be something that flows in a good order and makes sense.*

- *Delivers on time. As I mentioned before, most ghostwriters are notoriously late. The key is to give yourself some leeway for personal problems that might interrupt your schedule. Don't overdo it either – shoot for a daily per page completion under what you really think you can accomplish. If you finish early – the client will be very impressed.*

- *Learns enough about the business that they can help brainstorm. If you're hired to write an eBook, for example, the client will be very impressed if, when he tells you he needs an opt in report but can't think of a topic, you come up with one off the top of your head! Try to learn about the client's niche so you can be of service and not make him think of everything.*

It's not all just about quality. The other aspects are just as important. If you start doing things that other ghostwriters fail to do, you'll quickly become the go-to person for content and you'll have a client waiting list!

Where can you find ghostwriting gigs? There are several different ways to approach this – three that you can combine or pick from.

The first way is for those on a budget. If you can't afford anything at all, then simple sign up for free in a forum like **Warrior Forum** (earndifferent.com/wf) or other place where marketer's hang out and start posting and interacting.

Get to know people there and spread by word of mouth the fact that you're looking to write for others. You can even approach some experienced marketers and offer to do a free page for them so they can test the waters with you.

The second method is to sign up on a site like Upwork (earndifferent.com/upwork)This is a bidding site where you'll set up a profile and portfolio and you'll bid on projects that are posted by marketers.

For example, a marketer may post a project for a 50-page eBook. You can then bid on it (maybe $350 to start you off with some good feedback ratings – more positive ratings mean more projects awarded to you). The project will be awarded to the person the marketer wants to hire based on bid amount and quality of portfolio.

The last method you can use to find work is to create your own website. It's not expensive to get a domain ($10 a year) and hosting ($10-20 a month). And then you could install a free WordPress (earndifferent.com/wp) blog on it and have an order form built in!

What do I need to get started? The only thing you really need is a portfolio. Don't worry – it doesn't matter if you've never had a single client. You can create a simple portfolio by creating excerpts for them to browse.

Have a page on your site or a document you can send to people that has half page articles inside on a variety of niche topics. You might choose something like this:

- *One health article*
- *One pet article*
- *One financial article (Forex, insurance, etc.)*
- *One relationship article*
- *One marketing article (it can be simple like "working at home")*

This gives them a sense of where your strengths lie and it shows them you're versatile – because remember, most of them will have multiple niche markets and prefer to work with ONE ghostwriter who can do it all!

Building Backlinks

Backlinks are considered off-page SEO (search engine optimization). Marketers like to have other sites linking in to their own domain because in the eyes of Google and other search engines, it makes it appear as an authority site.

People will pay you to build backlinks for them and it's often quick and easy work – such as creating a profile in a forum and on the profile page, making a hyperlink that points to their domain.

Blogging

Many marketers love the fact that a blog feeds content to Google and other search bots on a regular basis. Frequent posting means frequent indexing into the search engines.

But blogging can be tedious. You have to whip up content, put it into the new post, format it, add any multi media like video embed codes, etc., and then publish it and ping it for the RSS feeds.

Customer Service

The big time marketers need all of the helping hands they can get. When their emails reach a flow they can't handle, then they'll look for a customer service rep who can learn the backend of their business and help meet the needs of their customers.

You can approach marketers individually or start some word of mouth buzz about being the go to customer service assistant for marketers. You'll need to compare pay on this one but it should be a salary or hourly wage.

Social Networking

It is virtually impossible for marketers to succeed without creating a sense of interaction with their niche community.

Marketers need things like:

- Facebook fan pages (earndifferent.com/fanpage)

- Twitter feeds (earndifferent.com/twitter)
- Hubpages (earndifferent.com/hubpages)
- Google+ (earndifferent.com/g+)

If you can go make a few of these to showcase your skills, then you might be able to create a service offering the social networking management of some of the most up and coming marketers out there.

Forum Population

Forum posts send a lot of traffic to marketers' websites. But the ones who are busy with product creation and networking can't sit there finding and building a reputation in forums. You can offer this service and make a bundle helping them build their brand.

Virtual Assistant

A VA, as they're known, does a little bit of everything. If the marketer has a 1-800 or 0800 number, then the VA might take calls for them. She might set up domains and register hosting.

Your VA services can be charged by the hour or per project – you have to decide what's right for you. And the great thing is, you can be a virtual assistant for more than one marketer at a time if the tasks allow for it.

Don't Let Services End Your Work at Home Journey

Some people start with a service, like ghostwriting, and continue writing until they finally retire. But what happens once you no longer want to work? Without a corporate retirement package, you may not be able to make ends meet.

So it's important that along the way, you make YOURSELF a client. All of those tasks you were offering to others – do those for a business model of your own that will provide residual earnings for you over time.

For example:

- *Pick an evergreen niche – this is one that will be around for an endless time, such as wedding planning or weight loss.*

- *Create an info product to sell to that niche market.*

- *Become an affiliate to cross promote other people's products.*

- *Set up joint ventures with other marketers in that niche*

The problem with most service providers is – they never make time for themselves. It's too easy to be tempted by money you can be paid RIGHT NOW by someone else than work toward something that will pay off *one day.*

We're going to cover some other business models that you can build. Maybe give yourself one day a week that's devoted to growing your own business. You don't want to work for every single dollar for the rest of your life – you want to have some income on autopilot.

Step 7: Plan Your Own Info Product Creation

Having your own info product is intimidating. You may question your expertise or think no one would buy an eBook from you – but you're probably wrong on all counts.

Print publications are slowly going the way of the dinosaurs – toward extinction. More people get their news and information online, or via their mobile electronic devices, such as iPads, smart phones, and ereaders.

This is bad news for media companies based in print, but it's wonderful news for people who can now self publish their creations without having to go through the grueling process of traditional publishing houses.

An info product can be created and sold on your own site, or you can put it on Amazon for print order (they'll print it on demand each time it's ordered). It can also be housed and available for Kindle readers.

So we're going to go over the main steps you'll need to know. You can dig down deeper into it if you decide this is a business model you want to pursue. But try not to neglect info product publishing forever – because it really enhances your authority.

Pick a Niche

First of all, I don't want you to think that old rule, "write what you know" applies here. The marketers creating their own info products often pick a niche they know nothing about – because you're going to be doing the readers a service as you create this guide.

Your lack of knowledge is sometimes a boost. If you know nothing about a topic, it means you (or your ghostwriter) will be digging into research – and your creation can be more up to date than someone set in his or her way of thinking about the topic.

So what niche do you write about? It helps to brainstorm a little bit. Start by doing the following and jot down a list that are possible niche topics for you:

- Go to ClickBank (earndifferent.com/clickbank) and view the marketplace to see what others are selling.

- Go to ClickSure (earndifferent.com/clicksure) and do the same.

- Go to Amazon (earndifferent.com/amazon) to see what non-fiction books are out there.

- Look at PLR stores (earndifferent.com/plr) to see what PLR topics are being produced (and if they show how many remain available, which ones are selling out).

- Off the top of your head, list a few topics you already feel that you know more than someone who knows NOTHING about it does.

- List some topics you WANT to know about, but don't know a thing about.

Narrow it down until you have a good niche topic you feel inspired about. Remember, you're going to be attached to this for a LONG time, creating a LOT of content for it – so don't choose something you think you'll burn out on quickly and easily.

Do Some Keyword Research

Now sometimes you'll think of a niche and you feel it's something everyone will want to know. But when you conduct your keyword research, you come to realize that no one is searching for information on that topic.

Keyword research shows you search volume. If there are zero searches, or too few, then it won't be worth pursuing this niche.

Go to your **free Google keyword tool** (earndifferent.com/planner) or, buy a paid keyword tool that will give you more detailed data if you have the funds available. Type in the broadest keyword or phrase you can think of for your niche.

For example, let's use "wedding planning" as your niche – the keyword you use might be "wedding" since it's the broadest one available. Type it without quotes and conduct a search.

Order the results for Global Monthly Searches from most to least. Start reviewing the keyword list to see what all people want to know about your topic.

With wedding planning, my list might look like this:

- *Attire*
- *Invitations*
- *Locations*
- *Rings*
- *Pictures*
- *Cakes*
- *Receptions*
- *Bands*
- *Favors*

And the list could go on for miles. But this quick list shows you the topics you'll need to have inside of your own info product. Then you organize the topics that flow logically in order and create your content from there!

Draft an Outline

It's best to work with an outline. You can have a chapter, and then create sub-headings – sort of like I'm using inside this very book. Feel free to put as many levels in your outline draft as you want to – but you can have nothing more than the main chapter headings if you prefer, too.

Let's use an example from above. Let's take Cakes as our example. Your chapter heading might be this:

"Wedding Cake Planning for the Bride and Groom"

You could have subtitles easily created just by going to your keyword tool again and looking up *wedding cake* to see what shows up. Make a list for subheadings like this:

- *Toppers*
- *Stands*
- *Photos*
- *Designs*
- *Bakery*
- *Price*

Then take that list and do another keyword search – let's look up the wedding cake topper for our next list and we get this:

- *Funny*
- *Custom*
- *Monogram*
- *Beach*
- *Cheap*
- *Military*
- *Firefighter*
- *Crystal*
- *Western*
- *Make your own*

When I saw this list, what I could do is group the items. So I might have a sub-section in this chapter about wedding cake toppers – and then separate the information into themes (where military and western might go), materials (where make your own and crystal might go), and custom (where monogram might be).

Keyword tools do a lot of the research work for you. You just have to dig down deeper and deeper and look at what the consumer's demands are.

Create the Product

This is where many would-be marketers freeze like a deer in headlights. You don't have to be scared. Let me take the pressure off of you – this info product creation stuff?

It can all be edited.

So if Joe Doe emails to tell you that you're the worst writer he's ever read because on page 13 of your eBook, you botched the spelling of a simple word – you just open up that Word doc, edit it, reformat it into a PDF and upload it.

Nothing's set in stone with this eBook stuff, so don't sweat it! Plus, I guarantee there are many other writers who are worse than you out there cranking out eBooks and making sales from them.

How long does your info product need to be? As long as it needs to be! Don't shoot for a blanket 50 pages or 100 pages. Just write until you've exhausted the information and you're sure your readers will be impressed and convinced they're not left with unanswered questions.

If necessary, you can outsource the product creation to a ghostwriter – but always double check the content inside to make sure they didn't steal it from someone else.

Turn It Into a PDF

You want to turn your document into a PDF file. This is the usual format for your info product. I also want to mention here that you don't have to create a text-based product at ALL!

In fact, if you want to use audio or video, go for it! But most people still use PDF content for info products, so that's where you can start the easy way.

You can use Adobe – either bought for your desktop or the online service version – to turn your Word document into a PDF file. Once it's converted, download it to your computer in a file where you know where it is.

Zip and Host It

Right click on your PDF file and choose "send to zip." Then log into your website hosting account and upload it in a product called something like 83756Products3862 so that hackers can't easily find your download area.

Put It on a Mini Site

Minisites are little one page websites that house a sales letter on them. They're designed with a header (the block at the top of your screen), a footer (located at the bottom), a background, a testimonial box, an eCover image, and an order button!

Look at almost any of the ClickBank (earndifferent.com/clickbank) marketplace products and you'll see what a minisite looks like.

You can create these yourself, but if you're not good at graphics, then the person who lands there might view you as unprofessional.

Minisites can range in cost from $100 packages to thousands of dollars. You can also go to Upwork (earndifferent.com/upwork) as a buyer and post a project and browse portfolios of designers to see if you can get something more in line with your budget.

Put It on Other Ordering Hot Spots

You're not restricted to your own minisite when selling your info product. Make sure you use Createspace to put it in the Amazon.com book section and add it onto their Kindle area, too!

Step 8: Plan to Tap Into Affiliate Marketing Earnings

So right now in your planning stages, you know where you can start with services or your own info product. But eventually, you'll want to add affiliate marketing to the mix.

Some people even start with this, but I believe it's vital to:

a.) Take the money pressure off with services that pay fast and...

b.) Launch your own product rather than having to rely on others to meet the needs of the marketplace.

Pick Your Niche

You have two choices here. You can go into the same niche as an affiliate you're in with your own info product. Or, you can pick a completely new niche to go into. Or even do a combination of the two!

The good thing about promoting as an affiliate for the niche you're already in is that you'll be building a list for that niche. So if you find another product that would meet their needs, sale would be easier to get with a group of proven buyers.

Don't worry if the product directly competes with yours. Many people buy up several resources on topics because they have unique viewpoints or teach methods a completely different way.

For example, let's say you were in the Internet marketing niche. Your guide teaches people how to get traffic to their site using free social networks. You build a list of 1,000 buyers who adore your strategy.

You could still later go to them and say, "I found a great product that teaches traffic via a paid route, which isn't what I teach, but something you may want to test out."

Traffic to their site could double and you've been the bridge that connected a prospective buyer to the seller, so you earn a commission from that (usually 50%, but sometimes more – or less).

Don't Ruin the Trust Your Followers Have in You

After you pick a niche, it means you have to pick a product (or several) to promote. This is where it's crucial that you have your subscribers' best interest at heart.

You may have the most honest and ethical product on the market, but not everyone does. So if you blindly promote anything, everything, and any*one*, it could ruin the reputation you worked so hard to create.

The only way to truly know if the product is worth recommending to anyone – subscriber or not – is to download it yourself and see if it has value. Many product owners will give you a free review copy if you just ask.

If you promote things just because there's a big launch happening or some buddy of yours asked you to (but you know it's not top quality), your followers will consider you less of an authority and your opinion will matter less and less.

Learn How to Write Reviews

Reviews can best be written when you're a real buyer who spent your own hard earned money on a product – and you implemented it and now want to share those results.

This is the same formula whether it's a dog training guide, weight loss eBook, or marketing course.

You don't want to share the secrets of the course – that wouldn't be a fair thing to do to the product owner, and you'd be shooting yourself in the foot with product sales.

But you can make a daily blog post as you implement something and chat about the results (or lack thereof) that you're getting. Talk about the good and the bad. Don't be afraid that pointing out the negatives will ruin your sales.

It actually makes your review more honest and realistic. And don't write up those phony negatives such as, "The only thing wrong with this course is that it ended and I want more!"

Your readers will see right through that.

Know How to Set Up Your Traffic Funnel

As an affiliate, I don't want you to send all of your traffic from the links you plan around the web directly to the product owner's sales page. This is a common mistake most rookie affiliates make.

What you want are long-term affiliate earnings. So follow me through this scenario:

You take the time to create a page on a blog in your niche. You write up an article, maybe make a nice video to go with it. You link directly to the sales page of the product you're promoting.

A visitor lands on your blog page from Google and sees the link on your blog. He clicks it and goes to the product owner's sales page and buys. You make a 50% commission.

Your relationship with this customer ends here. The product owner, however, has the customer's email address and can continue marketing to him or her for years to come.

Now let's look at a different scenario:

You take the time to create a page on a blog in your niche. You write up an article, maybe make a nice video to go with it. You link somewhere in the article to a page that has a freebie for your visitor if they enter their name and email address.

A visitor lands on your blog page from Google and sees the link on your blog. He clicks it and goes to YOUR squeeze page. He wants that freebie and enters his name and email address.

A few days later you email him with a warm message and a link to the product that you want to promote. He clicks through (because your freebie was so good that he trusts you a bit). He buys the product and you get 50% commission.

The monetary result is somewhat the same – you get that 50% commission. But instead of the product owner enjoying your customer's buying abilities for the rest of their time spent interested in this niche, you BOTH get the honor of communicating with the customer.

You can go on to recommend more products to them and increase the value of that one lead from a single sale to possibly dozens. It's far easier to work with an established list than to try to scrounge up new leads on a daily basis.

Watch Conversions and Refunds

You don't want to blindly promote things without knowing how it's working for you. Conversions are how well (or poorly) your traffic converts from a click through into a sale.

For example, if you make 1 sale for every 100 people you send to a site, then you have a 1% conversion rate. A decent one is said to be 2-4% but some products will give you a 30% conversion – especially if you've developed a good relationship with your subscribers or readers and they trust your opinion.

If a site isn't converting at all, then you may want to find someone else's product to promote. You can still use the same content – but just swap out the affiliate links to point to the new item.

Just as you watch conversions, you also want to watch refunds. If you're enjoying a nice conversion and suddenly your refund rate is soaring through the roof, you need to find out what the problem is!

If you reviewed the product and it was wonderful, then the problem could be coming from elsewhere. It could be that the product owner isn't supporting his buyers properly.

Maybe he doesn't answer support emails, or doesn't deliver on some of the promises he made in the course. If so, drop him like a hot potato after telling him what's wrong and giving him the opportunity to make it right.

Or perhaps he gets your subscribers on his list and then bombards them with daily product promotions of his own as an affiliate – which angers your list and makes them refund their purchase completely.

Again, contact the owner and tell him what the source of the complaints is after polling your subscribers to get their feedback. If he won't change, then make him suffer the loss of an affiliate.

Set Yourself Up to Have Product Owners Coming to YOU

Just because you're an affiliate, it doesn't mean you can't be THE go-to person in your niche as an affiliate. If you grow your review site of products big enough, you'll have people begging you to review their product – sometimes for a fee they'll pay you on top of the affiliate commissions, too!

Just don't get blinded by money and accept offers to review things in a less than 100% honest manner. Your subscribers and readers come first. Take care of them and they will reward you with their loyalty by purchasing through your link.

Step 9: Plan to Include Ad Revenue in Your Business

When you're doing things like blogging about your products (or someone else's), there's going to be room in the sidebar area for you to put things. Some people put an opt in box there, links to their social networking profiles, or hyperlinked images to the products they sell.

But don't forget about using the space for ad revenue, too. Blogs in particular can be high traffic entities, so publishers and product owners love the idea of placing their ads on your blog.

Most people know these are not personal endorsements by you. If anyone asks, just be honest and let them know that's a paid ad spot. There are two methods you can use to fill the ad space in your blog – or static website – AdSense and Direct Sales.

It Just Makes Good AdSense

This is a very quick and easy way to get ads set up on your website. AdSense (earndifferent.com/adsense) is a program owned by Google where product owners pay people like you have their ads on your site.

You don't get a flat fee, but rather earn money for every instance when a visitor on your blog clicks through to the product owner's site.

The money you earn depends on what the topic is. Some topics pay a lot of money per click (like insurance, for example). Others pay just a few cents – which can add up if you have a lot of targeted traffic.

You have to be careful to follow all of the rules that companies set up for AdSense earnings. You can't, for example, *tell* people to click on your link. That's considered fraud!

To get signed up, you'll go to Google's AdSense program and enter your domain and other info, such as what language your site is in. You'll agree to some terms and then enter the method for which you want to get paid.

You'll get paid once a month – via check or direct deposit into your bank.

You also have some semblance of control over what ads appear. For example, you can filter out certain competitive ads if there are companies you don't want siphoning off your blog traffic.

Once your account is approved by AdSense, you'll be ready to place your first set of code on your site.

Here's how to get your code prepared:

- *Click on AdSense Setup*
- *Choose what kind of ads you want – AdSense for content, search, RSS feeds, domains, mobile content, or applications. To put ads on your site, choose AdSense for content.*
- *Choose the Ad unit – you have the option to ask for text only, image only, or a mix of the two or go with*

the Link unit, which is a series of hyperlinks placed on your site instead.

- *Choose which format you want. This indicates the size and position of your ad. Do you want a large horizontal banner or a small button? Something in between? A nice vertical box? Choose whichever size you want on this step.*

- *Pick the color pallet that best matches your site. You want it to blend in nicely. Or, some marketers like it to stand out and be more noticeable.*

- *Choose the font options you prefer.*

- *Pick the corner styles (do you want the ads rounded on the corners, or square?).*

- *Make a decision about what you want AdSense to do if there are zero relevant ads to run in that space. For example, you can have them show a blank space, show some other ads that aren't from Google, or fill in the space with a solid color.*

- *Next, add a channel with your domain name so that you can see where the clicks are coming from. This may not matter if you only have one site, but once your business grows into something with multiple domains, you'll want to know if one site is outperforming all others in AdSense revenue.*

- *On the last screen, click the Submit and Get Code button. The code you see there will be copied by you.*

Once you have your code, it'll be time to get it strategically placed on your blog or site. Here are the instructions for loading the code into your blog so that it shows up in a sidebar:

- *Go to your blog and log into your dashboard.*

- *Click Appearance and then Widgets*

- *Drag a Text widget over to your sidebar (you can drag this around if you decide you want it placed somewhere else).*

- *Paste the code you copied from AdSense into the text widget and save and then close the widget.*

- *Check your site to see if there's a block of space there. The ad won't show just yet – you can come back later to see it once it's gone live. But you should see a blank area.*

Never, ever, ever click on your own ads. And don't ask others (your parents, cousins, and long lost friends) to do it, either. Google will ban your account in an instant and there's almost no way to ever get it back.

Selling Ad Space on Your Sites

Selling ad space will usually be an option once you get your traffic flowing in on a regular basis. Ad buyers will want to see stats of your site – and you can usually prove this by using a free tool called Google Analytics (earndifferent.com/analytics).

You can sell ad space in your sidebar, for example. You'll do the very same thing in order to place the ad that you did with AdSense, only you'll have the customer give you the code.

They may want a text hyperlink or an image ad.

Don't let them have control over exactly what's in the ad – set a few parameters. For example, you may restrict racy images for a dating site ad if you have an innocent parental site.

And don't let them include text on the ad that makes it look as if it's a personal recommendation coming from you.

What do you charge?

For this question, it's going to depends on many factors – not just traffic. You're going to want to see how competitive pricing is for ads in your niche. You might even contact some competitors of yours and ask them what they would charge for ad space.

Because traffic is what ties all business models in the Internet marketing world together, it's important that you learn as much as possible about pulling in the right kind of visitors, so let's move on to that topic now.

Step 10: Plan Your Traffic

Traffic is the holy grail of Internet marketing – if you know how to get it, then you can probably find a way to succeed in Internet Marketing. Problem is, everyone wants it to just "happen" and no one wants to work for it.

We're going to go over a great plan of attack for your traffic needs. You can pick and choose from methods you prefer and combine whatever you want. The only thing I ask is, try to test each method at least once – just so you know what worked and what didn't with your niche needs.

Get a Traffic Strategy in Place

Keywords are extremely important for getting traffic to your site. This is how you *pull* traffic into your site. When Googlebots come to index your site, they're going to be analyzing it for keyword usage.

You never want to stuff a lot of keywords purposely because you can get penalized by the search engines for doing that. But you do want to be strategic about it.

Keep a spreadsheet where you track the various keywords you've used in your blog posts. When you have an idea for a post, visit the spreadsheet to see if there's a keyword phrase that would fit in nicely.

For example, let's say you were in the dating niche. You want to do a blog post about how older women are now dating younger men quite often now. You look in your spreadsheet and see the phrase "cougar dating" has over 60,000 monthly global searches – so work that into your title and a couple of times in your post.

Blog frequently to make the most of your traffic abilities on your site. Google and other search engines love blogs and they will time their visits to your site based on how often you post.

For example, they might start off coming around every 3 weeks. Then they see that you're posting weekly – so they decide to come weekly. If you post daily, they'll come daily. And if you post several times a day, they'll be roaming your blog and able to index your new posts in mere minutes.

Indexing, by the way, means your page is now findable in the search engine. So if you're posting a lot and you make that new "cougar dating" post, your page could be the one chosen to be shown at the top of the SERPs in a very short period of time.

Google+ (earndifferent.com/g+)

Easy and free to sign up for - just set up an "About" page in your profile, and interact with people in your niche!

Remember, it's important not to be a spammer on ANY of the social networking sites. Do your best to be a valued member who contributes to the discussions and provides thought-provoking information yourself.

It's a mix of all sorts of networking features. You can even hold a video chat on the site where you and your target audience all "hang out" together on video!

Facebook (earndifferent.com/fb)

Facebook has a variety of traffic options for you to take advantage of. It's against the terms of service to have more than one profile page. But that shouldn't stop you from having a business fan page!

Create a fan page for people to "like" and that way they can follow you on their wall. You need to keep updating your fan page frequently, though – or the traffic will die down and your page won't be useful.

A fan page lets you post links, videos and pictures just like you would on a blog. But it's not the only way to build a traffic stream from the site. You can also opt to use their paid advertising feature.

Ads on Facebook are nice because you can choose the location, age and interests of the people you target. If your product is only applicable for people in America, then you can filter it so that it doesn't show the ads to UK Facebook users.

You set a daily budget and pay only when someone clicks through on the ad. This is similar to the way you *earned* money by placing AdSense ads on your blog or website.

Twitter (earndifferent.com/twitter)

Some people mistakenly ignore Twitter because they worry about how much marketing they could do in just 140 characters. But the reality is – a lot of traffic can come your way through Twitter!

Not only can you post messages (including links) to your Twitter stream, but those messages can get Retweeted to more people if your followers hit the Retweet button for you.

Make sure you treat your Twitter followers the same way you would followers on other social networks. Watch the feed and interact with them on their posts. Retweet some of their posts, too.

Don't *just* market to them. Have a good mix of personality in your Twitter stream to create a stronger brand loyalty. Let them get to know the person behind the account.

LinkedIn (earndifferent.com/linkedin)

LinkedIn used to be known as a social network to conduct job searches and network more within the corporate realm. But it can be so much more than that for you.

Fill out your complete LinkedIn profile and make sure you include a viral freebie download on it to help build a bigger following. People will look to see who's linked to who, and you'll see your contact list grow quickly.

Bookmarking Sites

Bookmarking is a great way to get your links shared by others. You can sign up for a bunch of different bookmarking sites, but start with one – like del.icio.us. You'll enter a link to a page on your site, post a short description, and add some additional information.

Others can see what you've shared. And then they too can share it. But you don't want to be viewed as a spammer. You want to create a healthy mix of link posts – bookmark some sites that aren't yours.

Other beneficial bookmarking sites include:

- StumbleUpon (earndifferent.com/stumble)
- Digg (earndifferent.com/digg)
- Reddit (earndifferent.com/reddit)
- Technorati (earndifferent.com/technorati)

Bookmarking can also be outsourced to people like virtual assistants. Or, you can sometimes buy a package that includes a certain number of bookmarks across the web.

Guest Blog Posting

You already know that blogging – and blogging frequently – is a boon to your sites when it comes to traffic. But you can also take advantage of other bloggers' traffic, too!

It's known as guest blogging – and bloggers are usually eager to take advantage of your offer! Bloggers have a hard time keeping up with an intense blog schedule when they have other tasks to complete.

So when an expert in their own niche comes along and asks if they can take over blogging duties for a day, it's a welcomed relief!

Start by finding blogs in your niche. Go to Google and type in your niche keyword. Let's start with the word *wedding* using a previous example in this guide.

When you search Google, look in the left sidebar of the results page and you'll see an option to just see the blogs available. Go to Alexa.com and click on the site tools tab. Then paste the site's URL into the tool. Click Get Details when the results pop up and you'll be able to see an approximate traffic profile for the site.

If it's a nice site with ample traffic, then go ahead and create a blog post that you feel would fit nicely on the site. For instance, if it's a "green weddings" blog, then come up with a blog post about a green wedding tip.

If you deliver an article that's not relevant to their niche – OR, not in line with what they teach, then it will prove to them that you didn't care enough to look their site over, and they'll decline your offer.

Deliver the content in both Word format and Notepad (TXT) so that they can quickly paste it into their site and schedule it for publications.

Make sure you include a bio blurb for the blog owner. This is something that comes before or after the blog post that tells a little about who the author is – with a link back to your domain. It shouldn't be too long – maybe 2 or 3 sentences, max.

Some blog owners will want to reciprocate with a guest blog on *your* blog, too. You can either accept this offer in good will or decline it, if you feel the message would hurt your site's credibility.

Forum Signature Files

If you participate in forums for your niche (which you should be, because that's where *real* people hang out), then you should check to see if the forum owner allows forum signature files.

A signature file is an area that automatically shows up below any post you make on the site. So if you reply to someone else's thread, it shows your message, with a sig file beneath it.

If you start a thread, your sig file shows up below that post, too. Some forums have rules for sig files – and some don't allow them at all. You might be able to use a mix of images and text, or one or the other.

Here are some other things to keep in mind if you're considering forum sig files:

- *You may not be allowed to use an affiliate link. If this happens, it's okay! Link to your own squeeze page anyway – just like the lesson you learned earlier about handing over a lifetime customer to someone else.*

- *You may have to wait awhile before your sig file shows up. Some forum owners know that seedy spammers come into forums to offer nothing of value – so they intentionally put a temporary hold on your sig file until you have a certain number of posts in the forum.*

- *Track, Test and Tweak your sig file until it converts into the most clicks it can get for you. Test out a variety of sig files – play around with the graphics or text and see what causes people to click on your sig file the most.*

- *Some forums have size restrictions for your sig file. They may be only 5 lines, or a specific width and height for images.*

The very best way to make use of your sig file is to provide good value to the forum. If people read a thread started by you and are amazed at its great value, they will often click on your sig file to see what *else* you have to offer!

Paid Traffic

Paid traffic can be a very scary thing for many marketers – even seasoned ones who have been around the block online for years! But you are in control, so don't let it intimidate you too bad.

Paid ads can be created through sites like AdWords. (earndifferent.com/adwords). Remember AdSense, where you *earned* money for ads placed on your blog? Well with AdWords, you're paying for your ads to be put on someone else's site!

In order to use AdWords, you have to know the rules. They don't mess around – so if you're caught breaking the Terms of Service, you could have your account banned forever.

Here are the basic steps involved:

- *Go to AdWords and create an account. This involved picking a username, picking a currency, verifying your account, and setting up billing information.*

- *Create a campaign for your AdWords account. First you're going to choose an audience. Where are they located? What language do they speak? Do you want to just advertise on Google SERPs or partner sites as well?*

- *Pick a daily budget. Warning: if you say you can spend up to $100 a day, they WILL find a way to spend your $100 a day. It's vital that you only spend as much as you can afford, period. Nothing more – or you'll go into debt very fast.*

  Now one thing to keep in mind – if your daily budget is just $20, and you're maxing out on that, look to see if the investment is paying off for you. Are those click throughs resulting in sales? If so, how much? How much can you afford to raise your daily budget?

- *Enter the maximum amount you're willing to pay per click. Some niche markets have keywords that cost a lot of money (think $50 per click!) and some cost just $0.05. Just because you put a maximum, it doesn't mean they'll charge that – and it also doesn't mean you get to beat out other advertisers for placement – there's more that goes into that equation than bid price.*

- *Enter a list of keywords associated with your site that you want your ad to show up for.*

- *Set up final billing data and your account is ready to go live!*

Now keep an eye on your ad campaign – don't let it get away from you. If your target page (the page you're sending people to) isn't optimized, you'll find out about it from AdWords.

Your ranking will fluctuate and you can tweak things in your campaign and on your site to get a better position in the SERPs. Paid advertising isn't ideal, but it does offer a quick start to some traffic flow for a new site with no foothold in Google yet.

Article Marketing

You're going to see a LOT of information about article marketing. Some of it is misleading, too. But it does have its merits so let's learn the basics of what you need to know about this traffic strategy.

Here are some tips that can help you maximize your article marketing efforts:

- *Know the rules! I know they're long and tedious to read, but it's going to take longer to get your content online if you ignore them, so just go through them once, jot down the important items, and then refer to them whenever you submit a new article.*

- *Decide if premium services are worth it to you. Some article directories are simply free. Others have perks for those who pay a monthly price – like faster article approval.*

- *Work on developing your call to action. This is the small area at the end of your article that gets people to click through to your link. Don't be boring and simply say something like, "for more information, click here," because that's not interesting enough to warrant a click!*

- *Spread your backlinking efforts among many sites – not just one. Many marketers use EzineArticles.com for their article marketing – but there are many others, like GoArticles – that you can use, too.*

- *Don't put all of your content on directories – save a good deal of it for your own blog and site!*

Article marketing can be done on a schedule that you create. You can outsource content to a ghostwriter and upload it under your name on the directories. Make sure it's unique so that it gets approved.

Once the article is live, use the proper procedures to publish the article from the directory onto your own blog or site!

Working at home for yourself doesn't have to be intimidating. You're going to feel SO much better once you have a plan in place to tackle the major aspects of building your own business.

Find someone to trust in your journey and rely on those individuals to help you or recommend products that are valid whenever you're entering a new area that's unfamiliar to you.

Conclusion

After reading this guide I hope you have a pretty clear picture of what working from home entails. As you've seen there are not only advantages, but most of the potential drawbacks can be mitigated with the right strategies and some experience.

What's important to remember is that working from home is not something that suits everyone. Some work better in an actual office setting where there is more social interaction and perhaps a better sense of being part of a "team", something that's not easily felt when working alone in your home office.

However, there's really no way of knowing which would work best for you unless you give working from home a shot. If you're interested in trying it but don't want to go all the way to being self-employed, talk to your boss and ask if you could work from home just one day per week. That will give you a taste of what it's like, and if you enjoy it and it works well, you can ask for more. Make sure you state the potential benefits, not just for you but also for the company (they probably mostly want to hear how you'll be more productive without the time wasted on a daily commute and distractions of the regular workplace). Before asking, take some time to think of good answers to all the potential questions you may get.

Of course, later on you may want to consider going self-employed instead, as that's when working from home really shows its true colors with complete freedom to do what you want, when you want. For most people it becomes a lifestyle, one that they wouldn't give up for anything in the world.

Are you ready to give it a go?

Dan Wiggs

London, England

P.S. Feel free to email me with any questions at dan@earndifferent.com

P.P.S. Keep a look out for my emails – you'll be getting some very cool free bonuses hitting your inbox within a day or two of opting in at earndifferent.com

BONUS:

The "High Commission" Secrets Of A Work From Home Millionaire MP3

The "High Commission" Secrets Of A Work From Home Millionaire MP3

I recorded this personal, one to one interview with one of the world's most succesful work from home millionaires earlier this year.

He reveals some eye-opening insider secrets, as well as the one simple but unexpected thing that you MUST do to succeed when working from home.

And it is is yours to download and keep – all I ask is that you tell your Facebook friends about *The "No Hype" Guide To Getting Started Working From Home.*

Visit the link below and follow the easy instructions to share - thanks!

earndifferent.com/unlock

Resources

Unmissable training resources and products that I've found vital in the setup and day-to-day running of my work from home business…

TIP: All the URLs referenced in this book can be found at <u>earndifferent.com/links</u>

<u>Live Training Event (FREE):</u>
IM Freedom Workshop

<u>http://www.earndifferent.com/imfw</u>

<u>Daily Training Videos (FREE):</u>
<u>http://www.earndifferent.com/insp</u>

<u>Online Training Courses (PAID):</u>
Make Money Blogging

<u>http://www.earndifferent.com/blog</u>

YouTube Secrets

<u>http://www.earndifferent.com/youtube</u>

Facebook Advertising Mastery

http://www.earndifferent.com/facebook

Instant Productivity Shortcuts

http://www.earndifferent.com/productivity

Google SEO Secrets

http://www.earndifferent.com/seo

CPA Secrets

http://www.earndifferent.com/cpa

PPC Advertising

http://www.earndifferent.com/ppc

Social Media Mastery

http://www.earndifferent.com/socialmedia

Direct Mail Mastery

http://www.earndifferent.com/directmail

Mastering Branding, Public Relations, & Social Media
http://www.earndifferent.com/branding

How To Create Ideas That Sell

http://www.earndifferent.com/ideas

How To Plan A Website That Attracts Profit

http://www.earndifferent.com/siteplan

Best Practices of High Performance Entrepreneurs

http://www.earndifferent.com/best

Achieving Work / Life Balance

http://www.earndifferent.com/balance

Affiliate Marketing Made Easy

http://www.earndifferent.com/affiliate

Email Marketing Profit Machine

http://www.earndifferent.com/email

www.ingramcontent.com/pod-product-compliance
Lightning Source LLC
Chambersburg PA
CBHW070808180526
45168CB00002B/535